Praise for *Please Be Patient, I'm Grieving*

"*After my wife died three years ago, I wish I'd had copies of this book to pass on to my friends. Too many advised me on how to grieve, how long to grieve, and things not to do the first year. They meant well; that didn't make them helpful. Like others who grieve, I had to find my own path to healing. Thanks, Gary, for this easy-to-read book. I hope many will read it.*"

—Cecil Murphey, New York Times bestselling author of more than 130 books, including *Gifted Hands: The Ben Carson Story* and *90 Minutes in Heaven*.

"*This book gives immense hope to the grieving heart and those who want to help. The author's simple, straightforward, and practical approach is refreshing and healing. I recommend it highly.*"

– Paul Casale, Licensed Professional Counselor / Marriage and Family Therapist

"*Another masterpiece for the bereavement library. This book is a must read for those who authentically want to assist and support those around us who are grieving.*"

–Dr. Craig Borchardt, President/CEO Hospice Brazos Valley

"If you've ever wondered how to help a friend who's grieving, Gary Roe has the answer. With comforting and practical words, Gary provides solid counsel for those who want to help the hurting but may not know how. He gives readers insight into grieving hearts and how we can support them in their time of need."

—Troy Allen, Senior Pastor, First Baptist Church, College Station

"Gary touches on a subject many people seem uncomfortable addressing for fear of hurting the grieving person more deeply. Please Be Patient, I'm Grieving succinctly explains the grieving heart's thoughts and needs. Thanks for this 'how to' Gary!"

—Carrie Andree, Licensed Professional Counselor

"Finally...a book for the grieving and those close to someone grieving! As a hospice social worker, this is a fantastic resource for patients and families. As someone who personally knows loss, this book provides great comfort. I could not recommend these words more!"

—Kim Dafferner, author / Hospice Social Worker

"This is an amazing resource for people who are grieving and for people around them. It's short and easy to read which makes it incredibly practical for people in the whirlwind grief causes. If you've ever wondered how to care for people in grief or how to let people know what you need in grief, this book is for you."

—Ann Smith, Reviewer

"This book touched on every raw emotion I have felt after the loss of my mother, sister in law and uncle over the past year and a half. The author likened grief to a bus that hits you unexpectedly and that is so true. This was a very comforting and easy book to read."

—Marcia E. Kelley, Author

"Having lost my own father and a friend in the last year - and having friends who have lost family members in the past year - this book has helped heal me from the pain of those who have pushed me away and has allowed me to fine tune the support I am giving my friends. I would recommend this book to both those who have suffered a loss, and those who want to support a friend or loved one in their grief. People often, in an attempt to help, actually compound the pain of loss through their words and actions. This book is a great resource to avoid the common mistakes that lead to pain."

—Virgil Lagasa, Author

"When my dad passed three years ago, I was suddenly thrust into a world that was so unfamiliar. First, I needed to deal with my own grieving. Then I really wanted to be supportive and caring for my mom. This little book would have been so helpful to have at that time. Authentic, easy to read, and so hopeful. Even three years after our biggest loss, this book has still been such a help."

—Janessa Kay, Reviewer

"Please Be Patient, I'm Grieving is a very important resource in helping support and care for anyone experiencing the grieving process. Knowing "HOW" to care for and comfort, as well as "WHAT" to do for loved ones, family and friends before, during and after the Remembrance Services. It's important to BE there for one another a day, a month and years afterwards."

—Dr. Maisha Tianuru

PLEASE BE PATIENT I'M Grieving

HOW TO CARE FOR AND SUPPORT THE GRIEVING HEART

GARY ROE

Thank you for taking grief and grieving hearts seriously.

As a companion to this book, we've prepared
a free, printable PDF for you called,

9 Principles for Caring for Grieving Hearts

Download your free copy today.

https://www.garyroe.
com/9-principles-for-caring-for-grieving-hearts

TABLE OF CONTENTS

OTHER BOOKS BY GARY ROE

Comfort for Grieving Hearts: Hope and Encouragement for Times of Loss

Teen Grief: Caring for the Grieving Teenage Hearts
(Winner, 2018 Book Excellence Award)

Shattered: Surviving the Loss of a Child
(2017 Best Book Awards Finalist)

Heartbroken: Healing from the Loss of a Spouse

(USA Best Book Awards Finalist, National
Indie Excellence Book Awards Finalist)

Surviving the Holidays Without You: Navigating Grief During Special Seasons (2016 Book Excellence Award Finalist)

Saying Goodbye: Facing the Loss of a Loved One

(with Cecil Murphey)

Not Quite Healed: 40 Truths for Male Survivors of Childhood Sexual Abuse
(with Cecil Murphey)

(Lime Award Finalist for Excellence in Non-Fiction)

To Jen.

I'm delighted to be with you in this adventure of learning to grieve well so we can love well.

You are truly amazing.

ACKNOWLEDGMENTS

Special thanks to Kathy Trim of TEAM Japan and Kelli Levey of Texas A&M for their expertise and assistance in editing and proofing this manuscript.

Thanks to hospice co-workers Kim Dafferner and Peggy Telg for their invaluable feedback and input.

Thanks to Hospice Brazos Valley President and CEO Dr. Craig Borchardt for his support and encouragement in developing resources to help grieving people recover, adjust, and heal.

Thanks to Glendon Haddix of Streetlight Graphics for bringing this manuscript to life with superb design and formatting.

Thanks to all those in the midst of grief who pleaded for a resource like this. *Please Be Patient, I'm Grieving* owes its existence to you.

OPENING REMARKS:

WHAT YOU WILL LEARN FROM THIS BOOK

Grief hurts. It's tough to go through, and painful to watch.

If you're reading this, chances are one or both of the following is true:

- Loss has hit someone you know. You sense their pain. You want to help, but don't know how. Perhaps you're concerned, even scared you will do or say the wrong thing and make matters worse. *What can you do?*

- You're grieving. It's like you've been hit by a bus and are lying in the middle of the road. You need help, but you don't know how to ask, whom to ask, or even what you need. You hunger for others to be with you and understand what you're going through. *What can you do?*

Please Be Patient, I'm Grieving is designed to meet these needs. It's written to help you better understand grief and discover what you can do – for others and for yourself.

In the following pages, I'll give you a look at the grieving heart – its thoughts, emotions, and struggles. If you're wanting to help someone who's grieving, you'll get a glimpse of what's going on inside and be better able to support them. In fact, you will discover nine ways to care for someone who's grieving and make more of a difference than you ever dreamed possible.

1

If you're in the midst of loss, you'll see yourself as you read, and be encouraged you aren't as weird or crazy as you may have thought.

WHY I WROTE THIS BOOK

My personal history of loss dates back to early childhood. The hits were many and significant. As I grew, my struggle to make sense of life and loss developed in me a passion for helping hurting people heal and grow. For the last three decades as a pastor and hospice chaplain, I've had the honor of walking with thousands through grief and pain. That led to books like *Heartbroken: Healing from the Loss of a Spouse, Surviving the Holidays Without You,* and now this volume.

I wrote *Please Be Patient, I'm Grieving* by request. Over the years, I've been asked repeatedly by those enduring loss to produce a resource for those closest to them. I've been told, "Please help them understand us!"

Hurting people need to feel loved – and that means being heard and understood. If we pull away, for whatever reason, they feel ignored, rejected, abandoned, even invisible. As months go by, they sense their lives and relationships changing. The initial loss was just the beginning. Now they're experiencing other losses too. The weight of the accumulating grief can be crushing.

We're all designed for relationship. When our hearts are broken, we need people in our lives we can trust.

This book is about becoming those kind of people – loving, understanding, and trustworthy companions willing to walk with others through hardship and pain.

WHAT YOU WILL LEARN FROM THIS BOOK

In *Please Be Patient, I'm Grieving*, you will learn...

- How your grieving friend, relative, or co-worker might be feeling and thinking.

- How to discover what they need and don't need.

- What to say and not to say.

- How to be a help and not a hindrance in their grieving process.

- How the grief and pain of others can affect *you*.

- How helping others stimulates your own growth and healing.

- How the skills discussed here can enhance *all* your relationships.

This book can help you develop a priceless ability– *how to hear the heart of someone who's hurting*. The benefits for them, and for you, can be staggering.

All this will be summarized into nine key principles. Apply these, and you will be better able to care for and support people who are hurting and grieving. You will also have more impact than you thought possible.

TAKE THE PLUNGE!

The grieving people in your sphere need you. This loss-ridden, hurting world needs you. You are more important than you know.

Thank you for being willing to take the plunge. The ripple effects could be huge.

Let the journey into the grieving heart begin.

CHAPTER ONE:

SHOW UP AND ENTER THEIR WORLD

"This is terrible. It's like my insides are being
put through a meat grinder.

Grief is deeper and more painful than I thought."

—Sophie

You can make a huge difference in the life of someone who's grieving. It begins by showing up and being willing to enter their world.

IMAGINE...

Imagine you've lost a close friend or relative. The news hits like a tsunami, knocking you senseless. You're stunned. The shock and pain are intense.

The people around you express sympathy, perhaps even empathy. You feel their concern. They say they will be there for you. You're counting on them, more than you know.

They go back to their routines. You can't. Your world has stopped. Your heart is broken. People are compassionate and give you permission to grieve – for about a month. If you're not back to normal by then, they wonder what's wrong with you.

You feel judged and belittled. You discover it's not safe to grieve. You try to hold it in, but it's eating you up inside. Powerful emotions surface and pound you without warning. Nothing is normal or routine anymore.

Those you counted on don't call or initiate. They look uncomfortable when they see you. You sense their impatience and disapproval. You feel them pulling away. You notice your relationships are changing.

This is awful. You didn't expect this. A new loneliness invades your heart. You feel sad, vulnerable, confused, angry – even embarrassed.

Grief is deeper, tougher, and more complicated than you ever thought it could be.

PEOPLE MAKE THE DIFFERENCE

Loss is painful. It crushes hearts, steals dreams, and destroys relationships. Grief can be terribly lonely.

Those who are grieving need us. *They need you.*

As a pastor and hospice chaplain, I've had the honor of walking with thousands of hurting people through the valley of grief. Watching their pain, recovery, and healing, I can say the following with great confidence:

People make all the difference.

When someone is hurting, the people around them are crucial. Some are helpful. Others are not.

People who choose to show up and be compassionate help grievers feel loved, accepted, and supported. Sadly, this is not the norm. What I hear most often from hurting people is that they feel misunderstood, embarrassed, judged, belittled, neglected, ignored, invisible, abandoned, and rejected.

This is not surprising. Pain is uncomfortable, and we typically don't deal well with it – whether it's ours or someone else's. We would rather skip grief altogether. After all, who wants to hurt?

Your grieving relative, friend, neighbor, or co-worker needs you. They don't want you to be superhuman. They don't need perfection. They don't want you to spiritualize the situation or try to make things better. Rather, *they're hungry for you to know what they're feeling and experiencing, and join them in it.*

They want you to enter their world and be *with* them, if you're willing.

UNDERSTANDING THE CHAPTERS AHEAD

The chapters that follow are divided into two parts. The opening sections are written in the first person. This is the voice of the grieving heart. It is a collective voice – written not as a quote from one individual, but rather a creative compilation of the statements of many.

This is your grieving family member or friend's voice. Read it with compassion and an open mind. Hear the cries of their heart.

The closing sections of each chapter are explanatory. These paragraphs are my attempt to describe how grief and the human heart interact, and what you can do to help, encourage, and support those who are hurting.

You can make a huge difference. Your presence and influence are more powerful than you realize.

A FEW THINGS TO REMEMBER

As you read, here are a few things to keep in mind.

This is not an exhaustive volume. This book is a starting point. Grief is a huge subject. It runs deep in our hearts.

This is not a perfect volume. Everyone is different and each individual's grief process is unique. Not everything in the following pages will be experienced by every grieving person. These pages are simply illustrative of most who have known loss.

This book is not a magic pill. True understanding comes from listening to another's heart and accepting what's found there. The content you're about to engage is designed to help facilitate deeper understanding and appreciation of the griever's heart. Relationships are complicated, and grief doesn't make them easier.

GRIEF TAKES GREAT PATIENCE

"Please be patient, I'm grieving." People in the midst of loss chose this title because grief takes great patience – for everyone involved. And the key to patience is understanding.

This is a journey to better understanding the hurting heart.

Listen.

Consider.

Stay open.

Reflect.

It's time to enter their world and begin to hear their heart.

"I want to support you. I will show up, and enter your world."

QUESTIONS FOR PERSONAL REFLECTION / GROUP DISCUSSION

Show Up and Enter Their World

1. What losses have you personally experienced? Which one was the most difficult for you to adjust to? How so?

   _____

   _____

   _____

   _____

   _____

   _____

2. Hurting people often feel belittled, judged, misunderstood, and rejected by those around them. Have you experienced something like this after a loss? What was that like for you?

   _____

   _____

   _____

   _____

   _____

   _____

3. When you think of the grieving people you will encounter in the future, what kind of impact would you like to make in their lives?

_____

_____

_____

_____

_____

_____

4. "I want to support you. I will show up and enter your world." Think of someone you know who's grieving. How might you apply this affirmation?

_____

_____

_____

_____

_____

_____

Know someone needing grief support?

Send them to www.garyroe.com

We're here to help. We care for grieving hearts.

"*Grieving is as natural as crying when you are hurt, sleeping when you are tired, or sneezing when your nose itches. It is nature's way of healing a broken heart.*"

—Doug Manning

CHAPTER TWO:

RESPECT THEIR PAIN

"The pain is deeper and more intense than I could have imagined.

It rattles my soul."

—Maggie

Loss is painful. It can be traumatic, even devastating. How we handle another's heart is important, especially when they're hurting. You can care for and support them by acknowledging and respecting their pain.

FROM THE GRIEVING HEART...

I'm hurting. Something traumatic has occurred. Someone I love is gone, and they're not coming back.

I don't know how to do this. It's like I've been hit by a bus, and I'm lying flat in the middle of the road, watching the sky go by.

The world speeds on, oblivious to my loss. I watch but can't seem to enter in. It's as if someone pushed the pause button on my life. My world has suddenly changed, forever.

I'm stunned. I'm hurting. My heart is crushed. Grief can be heavy.

And yet, I can't fully accept it somehow. This can't be real.

I know this is confusing for you. It's confusing for me also. You're probably wondering what to say or what to do.

You can come sit beside me in the road, if you want. You don't have to say much. In fact, you don't have to say anything at all. Your presence is worth all the words in the world right now.

I probably won't say much either. Don't expect much out of me. I won't be myself for a while. In fact, I may never be the same again. This is something we'll both have to grapple with, but now isn't the time for that.

Sometimes all I can do is lie here and breathe. I won't be here forever, but it's where I am today.

This is hard. It hurts.

I don't know how to begin, so I'll just stumble forward and hope my seemingly random thoughts and emotions will make some kind of sense to you.

Thanks for reading this. I know this is strange. It's weird for me, too.

Please he patient with me. I'm grieving.

GRIEF HURTS

Losing a loved one is painful and traumatic. It can wound the soul and crush the heart.

We lose parents, siblings, relatives, friends, co-workers, and even children and grandchildren. We lose people to death, divorce, moves, disasters, or illness. We can lose them in an instant, or we can lose them over time.

Unfortunately, loss is a huge part of life. How we deal with it makes all the difference – both for ourselves and those around us.

Your grieving relative or friend is hurting. Their "normal" is gone. The disappearance of someone they love is affecting them deeply.

- Change has hit their heart and life. You may not feel or understand it, but their pain is very real.

- It really feels as if they've been hit by a bus. Life is no longer business as usual for them.

- They need people who will be with them through this. Grief is lonely, but no one should have to endure this spot in the road alone.

- Helping them may be different than you think. They need people who will hear their heart and meet them where they are. And where they are is different for every person.

They're hurting. They're supposed to be. *Acknowledge and respect their pain.* They're getting hit over and over again. Venture out and sit beside them in the middle of the road. Your presence can be more comforting than you realize.

Grief hurts. It's emotional. Grieving hearts experience many ups and downs. Riding this emotional roller-coaster can be challenging, frustrating, and exhausting. We'll talk more about this and how you can help in the next chapter.

"You're hurting. You should be. You lost someone you love. I will respect your pain."

QUESTIONS FOR PERSONAL REFLECTION / GROUP DISCUSSION

Chapter Two
Respect their Pain

1. What struck you the most about what the Grieving Heart had to say in this chapter? Why?

_____

_____

_____

_____

_____

_____

2. Have you ever been hurting and someone didn't acknowledge or respect your pain? What was that like for you?

_____

_____

_____

_____

_____

_____

3. If your "normal" was suddenly gone, what are some things you would want or need from those around you?

_____

_____

_____

_____

_____

_____

_____

4. Think of someone you know who's hurting. How might you acknowledge and respect their pain?

_____

_____

_____

_____

_____

_____

"I am feeble and utterly crushed;

I groan in anguish of heart.

I am worn out from my groaning.

All night long I flood my bed with weeping

and drench my couch with tears."

—King David (from the Book of Psalms)

CHAPTER THREE:

ACCEPT THEIR EMOTIONS

"Where did all these emotions come from?

And what do I do with them?"

—Stephen

Grief is emotional. The grieving person's heart has been hit, and they will most likely be more emotional than usual. This is natural and normal. You can care for and support them by being aware of this and accepting them as they are.

FROM THE GRIEVING HEART...

My emotions are all over the place.

I'm sad. At times the sadness is so intense I can hardly think. It's a cloud overhead I can't see through. It's a tightness in my chest, a lump in my throat. It weighs me down. My shoulders sag. My head is heavy. It presses on the back of my eyes.

There are moments I'm sure I could flood the room with tears.

I'm anxious, even fearful at times. I've never been here before. I've had other losses, but this one is different. My heart is riddled with questions: What does this mean? How will I get through this? What's next for me?

I'm scared. I feel shaky.

I'm confused. Are these crazy emotions normal? What are others thinking? Am I going to come out of this in one piece?

My head is spinning. I get overwhelmed even while tackling the smallest things. I feel as if I have less and less space inside me.

I get angry. Why did this have to happen? Why now? Why us? Why me?

How dare my loved one leave! We weren't done yet! I wasn't done yet! And where was God?

I struggle with guilt. Things I said and didn't say. Things I did and didn't do. Mistakes swim before my eyes. Past pain has invaded the present.

I'm often numb. At times I feel nothing at all. My heart shuts down. I'm stunned. Paralyzed.

I'm a mess. Will I ever get it together?

Please be patient with me. I'm grieving.

GRIEF IS EMOTIONAL

Grief is an emotional process. When loss comes, it hits the heart. Hard.

Everyone has a natural balance of emotion and reason. This balance is different for all of us, influenced greatly by our backgrounds, experiences, and personalities. When grief strikes, emotion surges forward and often hijacks the heart. Multiple, seemingly contradictory feelings can assault us all at once. Emotion now occupies more space, and reason gets squeezed.

Many describe grief as an emotional roller-coaster. It's unpredictable, unnerving, and bumpy. Most roller-coasters last a few minutes. This one has no time limit, and it's anything but fun. Feeling overwhelmed, maxed out, or numb is often the result.

Triggers are everywhere. Places, people, fragrances, foods, music, seasons, holidays - almost anything can cause memories of departed loved ones to surface. The accompanying emotions can sweep over us in an instant - anywhere, anytime.

Those in the midst of grief have not only been hit by the bus – they get run over by it again and again.

It's not only the departure of the person that's difficult, but all the other losses that begin piling up as well. The future has changed. Certain goals, dreams, and plans are no more. Relationships will feel the weight of the loss too. The collateral damage can be staggering. This is painful, sad, and often produces anxiety and fear.

Altogether, the emotional upheaval is enough to make a person feel crazy.

Make no mistake. Loss is tough. It hurts. Emotions explode and leak all over the place.

ARE THEY MORE EMOTIONAL?
BE ENCOURAGED!

If the one grieving is more emotional than before, be encouraged. They should be. This emotional roller-coaster is natural and normal for grief. Your friend isn't crazy, but they are in a crazy situation compared to their usual routine.

They may be having trouble accepting themselves in this emotionally confusing state. Don't try to talk them out of their feelings. It won't work. Resist the temptation to try and make them feel better. You won't be able to. Instead, *accept them where they are, with all those nutty, up-and-down emotions.* If you can, it just might help them accept themselves.

With all the emotional upheaval, they probably don't feel or act like themselves. In cases of heavy, close losses, they might even question who they are now and why they're here.

What can you do? We'll address that in the next chapter.

"Grief is emotional. No wonder your feelings are all over the place. I accept you as you are."

QUESTIONS FOR PERSONAL REFLECTION / GROUP DISCUSSION

Chapter Three
Accept their Emotions

1. What can you relate to most in what the Grieving Heart shares in this chapter?

   _____

   _____

   _____

   _____

   _____

   _____

2. Which emotions are hardest for you to accept in your own life? Which emotions do you seem to have the most difficulty accepting in the lives of others?

   _____

   _____

   _____

   _____

   _____

   _____

3. Think of a loss you've experienced. What was some of the collateral damage that occurred from that loss (hopes, dreams, plans, the future, etc.)?

_____

_____

_____

_____

_____

_____

4. Think of a time when you were hurting badly and someone tried to talk you out of your emotions. What was that like for you?

_____

_____

_____

_____

_____

_____

Help us reach and care for more grieving hearts.

Share this link: https://www.garyroe.com/please-be-patient/

Together, we can make a difference in many lives.

"No one ever told me that grief felt so like fear."

—C. S. Lewis

"Grief is not a disorder, a disease or a sign of weakness.

It is an emotional, physical and spiritual necessity, the price you pay for love.

The only cure for grief is to grieve."

—Earl Grollman

CHAPTER FOUR:

GROW WITH THEM AS THEY CHANGE

"Pieces of my heart are missing.

I don't know who I am anymore."

—Paula

Grief affects relationships. For those grieving, this can be scary, even frightening. Some people disappear. Others draw closer. New people come into the picture. All this change can be overwhelming. You can make a difference by appreciating this upheaval and growing with them as they heal.

FROM THE GRIEVING HEART...

I'm not sure who I am now.

I know that sounds strange. You might say I'm who I always was.

But I'm not. I'm different. Loss has changed me.

I had a unique relationship with my loved one. It was ours, and no one else's. Yes, others are grieving too, but their grief isn't the same as mine. I'm not them, and they're not me.

Because my relationship was one-of-a-kind, my grief is unique too. My grief is mine alone.

This is a lonely road. I'm slowly learning to accept this.

This doesn't mean I want to be alone. Yes, I need time to myself. But I also need to stay connected to others who care about me – people like you.

You couldn't stop this bus from hitting me, and you can't stop it from running over me again and again. This is my grief, my bus, my road.

I don't know who I'll be when I finally stand up again. I don't know who I'm becoming. I don't know if you'll still like or love me, or whether I'll even like myself.

My world has turned upside down.

I'm upside down.

I have a hole in my heart where my loved one used to be. I have no idea what life will be like without them. Perhaps I can experience healing even with this hole in my heart. I hope so.

I'll have to rediscover or perhaps redefine who I am. I know I can't stay the same. Nothing is the same now.

But I don't know who I'll be. This scares me.

Please be patient with me. I'm grieving.

GRIEF AFFECTS RELATIONSHIPS

Life is about relationships - who we're connected to, how, when, and to what degree. People make all the difference in our lives, one way or the other.

When someone exits, it affects everyone they were attached to. For some the effects are subtle and hardly noticeable. For others the impact is massive, altering life's direction and dramatically changing relationships.

Because grief affects our relationships, it jostles our concept of who we are. It strikes at our identity and causes us to wonder why we're here and what life is all about.

Depending on the loss and the relationship involved, this identity crisis can be confusing, upsetting, and even traumatic. But it's also natural and normal. Eventually, we learn to somehow live again with a hole in our hearts.

YES, YOUR RELATIONSHIP WILL CHANGE TOO

Perhaps you sense your friend, co-worker, or relative is changing. That's hard because deep down you know this means your relationship must also change. This doesn't have to be negative or come between you. In fact, you have an opportunity to heal and grow with them, having an even stronger relationship in the future.

But it won't be the same. It can't be.

Grief changes us.

The choice is yours. You can grow together through this or choose to drift apart.

Grow with them as they recover and heal. You can make more of a difference than you ever thought possible.

What does growing together in grief look like? More on that in the next chapter.

"I want to be in this with you. I don't know who I'll become either. I'll grow with you as you heal."

QUESTIONS FOR PERSONAL REFLECTION / GROUP DISCUSSION

Chapter Four
Grow with Them as They Change

1. What touched you the most about what the Grieving Heart had to say in this chapter?

_____

_____

_____

_____

_____

_____

2. Think of a heavy loss you've experienced. How did your life change as a result?

_____

_____

_____

_____

_____

3. In the loss you thought of, how were your relationships impacted?

_____

_____

_____

_____

_____

_____

4. Think of someone you know enduring a loss currently. How can you grow with them as their lives change?

_____

_____

_____

_____

_____

_____

"For in grief nothing 'stays put.' One keeps on emerging from a phase, but it always recurs.

Round and round. Everything repeats.

Am I going in circles, or dare I hope I am on a spiral?

But if a spiral, am I going up or down it?"

—C. S. Lewis

"Trying to rediscover who you are is hard when part of you is missing."

—L. Robinson

CHAPTER FIVE:

SHARE THEIR LONELINESS

"People say they know what I'm going through.

No, they don't. They can't."

—Carter

Grief is lonely. No one knows exactly how the griever feels. It was their relationship and their loss – theirs alone. You can care for and support them by respecting their grief and sharing their loneliness.

FROM THE GRIEVING HEART...

I feel alone.

They said they would be there for me. They looked me in the eye and sent the message that I could count on them.

At least, that's what I heard.

But they haven't called, visited, emailed, or attempted to make contact. It's like they just vanished.

If I happen to run into them, a look goes across their face that resembles fear. Is there something wrong with me? When did I become scary?

I wonder what they're thinking. What do they think of me? Am I that uncomfortable to be around?

I don't want to be a downer. They probably have enough to tackle without me and my roller-coaster emotions.

Maybe something is wrong with me.

Sometimes I'm scared to go out. Bursts of grief slam me at unpredictable times and I find myself weeping in the strangest places. I feel like an embarrassment to myself and others.

Some have pulled away. Others try to fix me. Many give advice. Everybody wants me to feel better and move on.

The hole in my heart is aching. It's not just losing my loved one, but all the other losses that have come as a result. Nothing is the same. I've lost my routine and a sense of normalcy. Expectations, hopes, and dreams have disappeared. I sense my relationships changing.

Grief has changed me, and it's affecting everything.

Sometimes I feel like a leper, like my grief is some kind of disease. I hadn't counted on the pain of loneliness too.

I'm hurting. I'm a mess. I'm not who I was. I don't know who I am or who I will become. I don't know what normal is anymore.

Please be patient with me. I'm grieving.

GRIEF IS LONELY

Recently I sent out a one-question survey. I asked people to share with me what they struggled with most in their grief process. Out of roughly 500 responses over 80% said, "Loneliness."

Loneliness is a state of mind and heart, and not necessarily a life circumstance. In other words, it's possible to be lonely while surrounded by people.

People can feel alone in a crowd, a small group, a conversation, a family, or even a marriage. Loneliness strikes when we feel misunderstood, judged, or belittled. It creeps in when we sense our hearts are at a different place from those around us.

Loss shakes us. The mind spins, while the heart frantically searches for solid ground in the midst of what feels like a free fall.

A family can experience a loss together, yet all of them still feel alone. Part of this is natural, because the loss is different for each person. No one fully understands another's thoughts or emotions.

Grief is lonely. Because life is about relationships and we're all relational creatures, we don't typically deal well with the pain of separation. Loneliness is *not* one of our goals in life.

RESPECT THEIR GRIEF

Even if your grieving relative or friend is an extrovert, they are most likely struggling with the pain of loneliness. Your job isn't to make this better or eliminate this sense of loneliness. You can't. But you can be aware of their pain and support them while they're feeling lonely.

You can sit with them in the middle of their road.

Here are a few things to remember:

- Don't try to pull them out of this (you can't).

- Respect their grief and know that pain is a natural part of healing.

- As you can and are able, enter their valley with them.

35

Yes, *you can share their loneliness*, even if you can't feel it. This can have more impact than you can imagine.

What does it mean to be with them and share their loneliness? Often it comes down to what to say or not to say, what to do or not to do. We'll discuss that in the next chapter.

"I know this is a lonely road. Can I sit with you for a while?"

QUESTIONS FOR PERSONAL REFLECTION / GROUP DISCUSSION

Chapter Five
Share Their Loneliness

1. Read again the words of the Grieving Heart in this chapter. What struck you most as you read?

   _____

   _____

   _____

   _____

   _____

   _____

2. List a few ways that grief can be lonely. Which one is the most powerful for you?

   _____

   _____

   _____

   _____

   _____

   _____

3. We have a hard time letting people hurt. Can you think of some examples of how we try to pull someone out of their pain?

_____

_____

_____

_____

_____

_____

4. How might you share the loneliness of someone whose heart is broken from loss?

_____

_____

_____

_____

_____

Do you know someone who seems stuck in their grief?

Check out our free resources at https://www.garyroe.com/free-2/

Feel free to share our site – www.garyroe.com. We're here to help.

"In the midst of a world that moves, I alone am still."

—Natsume Soseki

"Everyone can master a grief but he that has it."

—William Shakespeare

CHAPTER SIX:

BE A SAFE PERSON

"People expected me to be better after a week.

Seriously? I may never be better, and I'll never be the same."

—Paul

Grief is deeply personal. What others say and do greatly impacts the heart and life of the grieving person. You can make a difference by being a safe person who has learned what to say and not say, what to do and not do.

FROM THE GRIEVING HEART...

How long is this going to take?

I sense I'm making progress and then, wham! Another grief attack comes, and it's like I lost them all over again. No matter how much time passes, it still seems like yesterday.

I've heard grief has no timetable. Honestly, I wonder if it will ever end. They are never far from my mind. I long for what was.

Please don't tell me to get over it. I can't. I don't want to. But I need to get through this time in the healthiest way possible.

Don't tell me I need to move on. If moving on means leaving them behind, forget it. I must find a way to go forward with them, somehow, someway.

Don't tell me they're in a better place. That might be true, but I want them here, now. Maybe that's selfish, but it's where I am sometimes.

Don't try to fix it or make me feel better. There is no fixing this. And there is no way out of the pain. Only through it.

Don't be afraid to speak their name and talk about them. They are precious to me. Ask me about them sometimes – what I love and what I miss. After all, it's not like I could forget them.

Don't push me into decision-making. I'm drained, emotional, and often confused. Now isn't the time for major, life-altering decisions. I've had enough change for a while.

Don't ask me what I need, because I don't know. You know me. You don't have to ask. Just do.

Time doesn't heal all wounds, but healing does take time.

I need time.

How much? I don't know. I'm not sure I'll ever heal completely, or that I even want to. I know I want to learn to live well with this hole in my heart.

So forgive me if I'm unpredictable, emotional, and different. I'm trying to live with this loss – somehow.

Please be patient with me. I'm grieving.

GRIEF IS PERSONAL

Grief is deeply personal. It's different for each person and each loss. To say such-and-such should happen, how, and when is, well, unrealistic.

Your grieving friend or relative is unique. There's no one else exactly like them. Their grief – how they view and handle this particular loss – is unique as well.

It's important to know that although many will go back to their routine after a short period of sadness, those deeply touched by the loss will not. Their routine is gone. It shocks and even angers them that others expect them to be better quickly.

One of the best things you can do for them is to be *a safe person*.

BEING A SAFE PERSON

A safe person:

- Doesn't evaluate, judge, or belittle.

- Doesn't try to fix the person or the situation.

- Accepts the grieving person as they are.

- Knows the greatest gift they can give is their presence.

- Listens to the griever's heart, not just their words.

- Has no agenda except to love the hurting person in the midst of their pain.

Honestly, safe people can be rare and hard to find. But you can be one. And this could make all the difference, not just to your friend, but to you as well.

Being in the presence of grief isn't easy. Walking with someone who keeps getting run over by a bus isn't what most of us dream about. But it's part of life and love. And what an honor to serve someone as we would want to be served.

Don't worry about what to say. Resist the temptation to fill the air with words. *Again, your presence is the most powerful gift you can offer.*

Be a safe person. Be salve to their wounded heart. Not only will you make more of a difference than you thought possible, you will also grow in ways you never imagined.

The grieving person often wonders if what they're experiencing is normal. You may be wondering that too. How can you help them with this? And when should you be concerned? We'll discuss these things in the next chapter.

"No matter how many times the bus comes, I'll be right here with you. I'll strive to be a safe and trustworthy companion."

QUESTIONS FOR PERSONAL REFLECTION / GROUP DISCUSSION

Chapter Six
Be a Safe Person

1. The Grieving Heart shared some deep thoughts in this chapter. Which of these thoughts have you experienced personally?

_____

_____

_____

_____

_____

_____

2. "Time doesn't heal all wounds, but healing does take time." How have you experienced the truth of this statement?

_____

_____

_____

_____

_____

_____

3. Reread the description of a safe person. Which of these points is the most difficult for you to live out?

_____

_____

_____

_____

_____

_____

4. Do you have at least one safe person in your life? Describe what it's like to be with them.

_____

_____

_____

_____

_____

_____

"Grief lasts longer than sympathy, which is one of the tragedies of the grieving."

—Elizabeth McCracken

"There is a time for everything, and a season for every activity under the heavens...a time to weep and a time to laugh, a time to mourn and a time to dance..."

—King Solomon (from Ecclesiastes)

CHAPTER SEVEN:

CONNECT THEM WITH OTHERS

WHO KNOW GRIEF

"Normal has disappeared. I don't know what that is anymore."

—Kathy

Grief impacts our thoughts, emotions, physical health, and spiritual well-being. Managing all the change involved is challenging. You can make a difference by helping grieving people connect with each other. This can be incredibly affirming and healing. In this chapter, you'll also learn some grief warning signs to be aware of and what to do should you see them.

FROM THE GRIEVING HEART....

Is this normal?

Life is anything but routine. Everything feels abnormal, surreal, and weird.

My thinking isn't as sharp. I forget things, appointments, even birthdays. I lose words and can't seem to express myself the way I used to. Focusing on anything is difficult.

My emotions are up, down, and all around. I'm more irritable and impatient. I'm moody and often zone out. Sometimes just staring at the wall feels good.

I get sick more often. I have strange physical sensations and symptoms. I trip and bump into things. I feel like a klutz. I'm tired all the time.

I question things I didn't before – deep, spiritual things. What really happens when we die? Will I see them again? How can God allow pain and grief like this?

Is this normal? I don't know. No wonder I feel crazy sometimes.

I can't do this alone. I need to find someone who knows. I don't know whether to be concerned about me or not. I need perspective.

Where can I find people who know grief?

I don't want to be a burden. I'm sorry.

Please be patient with me. I'm grieving.

GRIEF AFFECTS THE WHOLE PERSON

When we get hit by the Grief Bus, it affects our whole person – our thoughts, feelings, physical health, and spirituality. Such all-encompassing change, coupled with the uniqueness of each person's grief process, can make it difficult to discern what's normal and what's not.

Finding and spending time with people who know grief can be immensely helpful and affirming. When others share their experiences, grieving people suddenly realize they're not alone, they're not crazy, and they might somehow make it through this.

Where do we find these people? Usually in support groups. These groups might be sponsored by a church, a hospice or healthcare organization, a grief center, or private individuals. Time with others who've been hit by the Grief Bus can be powerfully comforting and reassuring.

However, for some the thought of going to a group can be intimidating. You can ease some of the pressure by offering to go with them to check it out. This small gesture on your part might make all the difference.

Encouraging your friend or relative to get around others who know grief can be huge for them. The impact could be extraordinary.

WHEN TO BE CONCERNED

How do you know when to be concerned? Here are a few red flags:

ISOLATION

Wanting and needing time alone is natural in grief. Withdrawing from busy schedules and activities is often helpful. However, if a person isolates to the point of almost never going out or interacting with anyone, there is probably cause for concern.

DEPRESSION

Depression on some level is common in grief. Many experience deep sadness, lack of motivation, listlessness, and fatigue.

But when the following occur, depression may be gaining a more serious foothold:

- Not getting out of bed for days

- Lack of motivation and interest in life

- Increasing withdrawal from people and activities

- General lack of self-care and hygiene

- Substance abuse (food, alcohol, drugs, etc.)

When a person ceases to be functional in everyday life, that's a signal professional help is needed.

SUICIDAL IDEATION

Some speak of wanting to go to heaven to see their loved ones. Others might say their loved one was their life, and they no longer know why they're here. This isn't unusual in heavy, close losses.

Here are some indicators that are more serious:

- They say they want to die, or no longer want to live.

- They talk about ending their life.

- They mention a weapon or suicide plan.

If these kind of thoughts are expressed, 911 or a suicide hotline should be contacted immediately.

Remember, it's not about getting it right or perfect. It's about showing up and accepting them where they are.

In this chapter, we talked about how important grieving people can be to one another. They can empathize, affirm each other, and give one another perspective. We also discussed some potential grief warning signs and what to do should you encounter them.

We've all experienced loss. We've been wounded, time and again. Sometimes another person's grief can trigger stuff buried deep in our own hearts. What do we do when this happens? We'll talk about that in the next chapter.

"Grief can be confusing. I'm glad we're in this together. Let's find others who know grief and can walk with us."

QUESTIONS FOR PERSONAL REFLECTION / GROUP DISCUSSION

Chapter Seven
Connect Them with Others Who Know Grief

1. In this chapter, the Grieving Heart shares how a life can be upended following a loss. Which parts could you relate to most?

_____

_____

_____

_____

_____

_____

2. We all need people who can relate to our loss somehow. Where and how can you find these people in your community?

_____

_____

_____

_____

_____

_____

3. Have you experienced some depression as a result of a loss? What was that like?

_____

_____

_____

_____

_____

_____

4. When hurting, we have a tendency to isolate. Have you seen this in your life and in the lives of others? How so?

_____

_____

_____

_____

_____

_____

"My eyes have grown dim with grief; my whole frame is but a shadow."

—The Book of Job, 17:7

"Be merciful to me, Lord, for I am in distress; my eyes grow weak with sorrow, my soul and body with grief."

—King David (from Psalms)

CHAPTER EIGHT:

LET THEIR GRIEF HELP YOU

HEAL AND GROW

"My grief is different than yours,

but that doesn't mean we can't walk together."

—Courtney

We all experience loss. We all know grief on some level. There are times when another person's pain can trigger our own. While we're trying to help others, stuff from our own past can surface and get in the way. You can better care for and support others by being aware of this and paying attention to your own heart. Their grief can help *you* heal and grow.

FROM THE GRIEVING HEART...

I know this is hard.

What's this like for you? The pain is immense. I know you care about me. This must be difficult to watch.

You've had losses too. Do you still feel them? Does your heart still ache?

We're not that different. Just as my past pain can invade the present, yours can too. Are you hurting? Perhaps we can comfort and encourage each other.

I know our relationship will change. I hope we can heal and grow together rather than drifting apart. To be honest, I'm terrified of more loss.

On the other hand, watching me get run over by this bus again and again can't be pleasant or fun. It's okay if you can't sit in the road beside me. I understand if it's too much.

I don't need you to be superhuman. I don't expect you to solve things for me or somehow make them go away. I want you to be you, whatever that means, in this situation.

Thank you for listening. It's a comfort knowing you care. If you think about it, pray for me. I need all the help I can get.

My world has changed forever. My heart hasn't caught up yet. Someday the color will return. For now, everything is pale and foggy.

My soul sighs a lot these days. I'm tired all the time. Even thinking is a chore. This is harder than I ever dreamed.

I'm glad now is not forever.

Please be patient with me. I'm grieving.

WE ALL HAVE A HISTORY OF LOSS

I recently asked some professional counselors how many of our struggles are related to unresolved grief. Their answers averaged out to a whopping 85%.

We all have a history of loss. We've lost people, homes, jobs, pets, possessions, health, and relationships. We've been wounded and also caused our share of pain. How we process what happens to and around us is critical.

How we handle loss shapes how we see ourselves, others, life, and even God. How we interpret what happens in life forms the foundation for the way we do relationships.

When you see your friend in pain, it impacts your heart. The grief might even trigger losses from your past. You are not a robot. You are a unique individual with a heart, mind, and soul.

In other words, their grief can be a gift. Because of your relationship, their loss becomes an opportunity for *you* to heal and grow.

BE AWARE OF YOUR OWN HEART

As you sit beside them in the road, be aware of your own heart too. What's happening in there? What are you feeling? *Perhaps the bus is running over you too.*

For your own sake, take some time to process:

- Is there unfinished business in your past?

- Are there things you need to revisit and resolve?

- Do you need to forgive or ask forgiveness?

- Are there amends that can be made?

If we're willing, loss can give us the gift of perspective. Experiencing grief gives us an opportunity to reconsider what should be most important in life. It can also motivate us to refocus on who we are and why we're here. And this can lead to healing, and possibly changes for the better.

YOU NEED EACH OTHER

Yes, your friend is hurting and needs you. You need them too.

Again, don't worry about getting this right or perfect. Grief is a moving target. Care for and support your friend or relative as best you know how and be patient with yourself along the way. Do this, and you will make more of a difference than you can imagine.

In this chapter, we talked about how another person's grief can affect you. Their pain can triggers yours. We discussed how you can use this as an opportunity to further heal from past wounds and losses.

Dealing with grief and loss requires great patience. In the process, we need to be patient with ourselves too. How? More on that in the next chapter.

"Grief is a tough and bumpy road, but we can walk it together. You are helping me heal and grow too."

QUESTIONS FOR PERSONAL REFLECTION / GROUP DISCUSSION

Chapter Eight
Let Their Grief Help You Heal and Grow

1. What struck you most from what the Grieving Heart shared in this chapter?

_____

_____

_____

_____

_____

_____

2. It can be hard to watch someone in emotional pain. What is it like for you when someone around you is hurting?

_____

_____

_____

_____

_____

3. Has another person's pain ever triggered your own losses and grief? What was that like?

_____

_____

_____

_____

_____

_____

4. We all have a history of loss. Is there unfinished business
   in your past? Are there things that need to be revisited
   and potentially resolved through forgiveness or making
   amends?

_____

_____

_____

_____

_____

_____

Do you have a question about grief or the grieving process?

Ask us. Visit www.garyroe.com and send us an email.

We'll be glad to help.

"Deposits of unfinished grief reside in more American hearts than I ever imagined. Until these pockets are opened and their contents aired openly, they block unimagined amounts of human growth and potential. They can give rise to bizarre and unexplained behavior which causes untold internal stress."

—Robert Kavanaugh

"Above all else, guard your heart; it is the spring from which everything else flows."

—King Solomon (from Proverbs)

CHAPTER NINE:

BE PATIENT WITH YOURSELF AND THEM

"What would I have done without those who showed up for me?

I'm here and healing because of them."

—Isabella

Grief will be expressed. We can attempt to run from or bury it, but it will leak out or burst forth anyway - usually in ways we won't like. Learning to be patient with ourselves and others can help us all grieve in healthier ways.

FROM THE GRIEVING HEART...

Hello again, my friend.

I'm still here, in the middle of the road. Yes, I'm still grieving. I think I always will be.

My loved one may be gone, but the hole in my heart remains. I will heal eventually, but not completely, and I certainly won't be the same. I hope you can understand this.

My grief could spill out at any moment, anywhere. The Grief Bus strikes without warning. I feel vulnerable, but I know that's part of the process. I'm hurting because I dared to love. And I'm so glad I did.

My heart is encouraged that you have read this. It gives me hope. I'm grateful you have been sitting with me in this road. I know you've seen me get hit again and again.

I'm not alone. I'm not crazy. I'm going to make it. I'll learn to live again with this hole in my heart.

Please keep being patient with me. I'm grieving.

GRIEF WILL BE EXPRESSED – ONE WAY OR ANOTHER

Grief is tough stuff.

Many try to ignore it, hoping it will disappear. Grief likes to move in, settle down, and make itself at home. *It won't simply go away on its own.*

Many attempt to run from it, perhaps hoping they can move fast enough to stay ahead of it. We can't outrun grief. *No one is that fast.*

Many stuff it deep down inside, thinking that if they refuse to feel the pain, they will somehow get past it. *People who have tried this will attest to the fact that it doesn't work.*

Grief ignored, stuffed, and fled from only gets stored away to be dealt with later. In the meantime, it leaks, often in insidious, unhealthy ways like substance abuse, physical illness, and mental and emotional disorders.

Grief is real, and it will be expressed. It is the natural and normal response to loss. As Doug Manning said, "It is nature's way of healing a broken heart."

PLEASE BE PATIENT WITH YOURSELF

Thank you for taking the time to better understand the grieving heart. Hopefully, you will find this helpful and encouraging as you encounter family, friends, and others who are getting hit by the Grief Bus.

This is hard for them, and for you too. *Please be patient with yourself. And thanks for being patient with them.* Do this, and who knows what might happen.

Not only will you make a difference in the life of someone you care about, you will grow in ways you never imagined.

"We're in this together. I'll practice being patient with myself too."

QUESTIONS FOR PERSONAL
REFLECTION / GROUP DISCUSSION

Chapter Nine
Be Patient with Yourself and Them

1. Reread what the Grieving Heart says in this chapter. What surprises or strikes you the most?

_____

_____

_____

_____

_____

_____

2. Grief stuffed or ignored only gets stored away to be dealt with later. How have you seen the truth of this?

_____

_____

_____

_____

_____

3. If you're grieving, how might you be more patient with yourself? How can others help you with this?

_____

_____

_____

_____

_____

_____

4. If you're in the presence of someone grieving, how might you need to be patient with yourself?

_____

_____

_____

_____

_____

_____

"The reality is that you will grieve forever. You will not 'get over' the loss of a loved one; you will learn to live with it. You will heal and you will rebuild yourself around the loss you have suffered.

You will be whole again but you will never be the same. Nor should you be the same nor would you want to be."

—Elisabeth Kübler-Ross

CONCLUSION:

WHAT HELPS IN GRIEF
OFTEN HELPS IN LIFE

"Why didn't I see this before? What helps in grief helps in life."

—Katy

In this book, you've gotten a glimpse into the grieving heart. You've heard some of the griever's pain, struggles, and questions. You've been introduced to nine ways to care for and support them in the midst of their pain. You've learned what to say and not say, what to do and not do, and what to watch out for.

Now that you've sat in the road with someone who's grieving, I want to challenge you to think even bigger.

MOST OF US ARE HURTING

Most of us are hurting inside. The pain can drive us more than we realize. It can keep us from moving forward and taking the risks necessary to fulfill our purpose. It can cause us to play it safe and settle in life, marriages, families, and relationships. Due to past wounds, we often pass on what's possible and opt for what's convenient and comfortable.

We're all in the midst of loss. We're losing things, possessions, abilities, relationships, hopes, and dreams all the time. This means that *you can apply the nine principles outlined in this book in any situation and relationship.*

1. Show up and enter their world.

What if you did this, on some level, even for a moment, with most of the people you meet? The impact would be astounding.

2. Respect their pain.

Look into someone's eyes long enough, and chances are you will begin to sense the hurt and struggle there. Allowing people to air their pain in your presence can be comforting and encouraging.

3. Accept their emotions.

If people can express what's inside without fear of judgment, it opens the way for all kinds of growth and healing.

4. Grow with them as they change.

People change when they go through pain. If you stick with them, it can help them adjust and experience some healing. And you can learn and benefit greatly from their experience.

5. Share their loneliness.

People are lonely inside. Keeping this in mind can greatly change what you say and do. You can help others (and yourself) live the truth, "You might feel lonely, but you're far from alone."

6. Be a safe person.

People are tired of being evaluated, belittled, and judged. You can offer safety and acceptance. Hearts begin to experience healing when people feel seen and heard.

7. Connect them with others who know grief.

Intentionally connect people with others who have what they need and watch what happens. Miraculous stuff can occur.

8. Let their grief help you grow and heal.

Be open to learn from the lonely, hurting people around you. The benefits will be extraordinary, both for them and for you.

9. Be patient with yourself and them.

Being patient with yourself and others can help us all fail forward. Having the freedom to fail frees people to risk, and ultimately succeed.

As Katy said at the beginning of this chapter, "What helps in grief often helps in life." Apply these nine principles in the midst of your routine and watch what happens.

Thank you for reading *Please Be Patient, I'm Grieving.* You've learned useful principles and skills that can enhance your heart and the lives of those around you. On some level, we're all hurting. If we're willing, we can care for and support each other and make a real difference in one another's lives.

Here's to better understanding and supporting the grieving hearts around us...

QUESTIONS FOR PERSONAL REFLECTION / GROUP DISCUSSION

Conclusion
What Helps in Grief Often Helps in Life

1. What do you think of Katy's statement, "What helps in grief, helps in life." In what ways have you found this to be true?

_____

_____

_____

_____

_____

_____

2. Look over the Nine Principles again. Which of these is the most difficult for you to apply at present? Explain.

_____

_____

_____

_____

_____

_____

3. Which of the Nine Principles is the most important for you personally right now? Explain.

_____

_____

_____

_____

_____

_____

4. In one statement, summarize the kind of impact you would like to have in the lives of those around you.

_____

_____

_____

_____

_____

_____

"Grief is a most peculiar thing; we're so helpless in the face of it. It's like a window that will simply open of its own accord. The room grows cold, and we can do nothing but shiver. But it opens a little less each time, and a little less; and one day we wonder what has become of it."

—Arthur Golden, *Memoirs of a Geisha*

FINAL THOUGHTS AND SUGGESTIONS

THINGS TO REMEMBER ABOUT GRIEF:

- Grief is a natural, normal, and necessary response to a loss. It's essential for healing a broken heart.

- Grief is powerful and emotional. It will be expressed – one way or another.

- Grief is an individual process, unique to every person and loss.

- Grief is unpredictable. It can hit the heart anytime, anywhere.

- Grief has no timetable. It takes as long as it takes. On some level, we may never stop grieving.

- Grief isn't an item to be checked off a list or a task to be accomplished. It's a process of learning to live on with a hole in the heart.

- Grief and loss are big parts of life. How we handle loss is important and influences our lives and relationships more than we realize.

Gary Roe

REMEMBER THE NINE PRINCIPLES:

1. *Show up and enter their world.*

   Meet them where they are. Show up, listen, and support without judgment or evaluation.

2. *Respect their pain.*

   Grief hurts. Appreciate their pain. Learn to hear their heart. Words are overrated. Your presence is the most powerful and precious gift you can give.

3. *Accept their emotions.*

   Grief can be an emotional roller-coaster. Enter their world, and accept them as they are, with all of their up-and-down emotions.

4. *Grow with them as they change.*

   Grief is changing them. Expect your relationship to change too. Choose to grow with them through this rather than pulling away.

5. *Share their loneliness.*

   Grief is lonely. Their loss is theirs alone, but you can be with them while they struggle. Open your heart and make yourself available.

6. *Be a safe person.*

   Grieving people need non-judgmental, trustworthy, and safe people who love them for who they are, where they are. Safe people have great impact.

7. *Connect them with others who know grief.*

   Being with others who are also enduring loss can be comforting and affirming. Grieving hearts need a lot of reassurance.

8. *Let their grief help you heal and grow.*

   Keep a watch on your own heart. Their pain may trigger some of your losses. This is an opportunity for you to heal from past wounds too.

9. *Be patient with yourself and them.*

   Grief requires patience. Be in this for the long haul. Give the gift of patience to both yourself and them.

Don't worry about getting this right or perfect.

Stay open.

Be yourself and be willing to grow.

Be as loving as you know how.

Don't try to be superhuman.

Take care of yourself. You're no good to others if you don't.

Look into their eyes and hear their heart:

"Please be patient with me. I'm grieving."

RESOURCES FOR THE GRIEVING HEART

BOOKS

Comfort for Grieving Hearts: Hope and Encouragement for Times of Loss

We look for comfort. We long for it. Grieving hearts need it to survive. Written with heartfelt compassion, this easy-to-read, warm, and practical book reads like a caring conversation with a friend and is destined to become a classic for those looking for hope and encouragement in times of loss. Composed of brief chapters, *Comfort for Grieving Hearts* is designed to be read one chapter per day, giving you bite-sized bits of comfort, encouragement, and healing over time. Available through Amazon and most major online retailers. For more information or to download a free excerpt, visit www.garyroe.com.

Teen Grief: Caring for the Grieving Teenage Heart

Teens are hurting. While trying to make sense of an increasingly confusing and troubled world, teens get hit, again and again. Edgy, fun-loving, tech-driven, and seemingly indestructible, their souls are shaking. We can't afford to allow pain and loss to get the better of them. Written at the request of parents, teachers, coaches, and school counselors, this informative, practical book is replete with guidance, insight, and ideas for assisting teens navigate the turbulent waters of loss. *Teen Grief* is a Winner of the 2018 Book Excellence Award and has received rave reviews from those who live and work with teens. *Teen Grief* is available in both paperback and electronic versions. For more information or to download a free excerpt, visit www.garyroe.com.

Shattered: Surviving the Loss of a Child

Unthinkable. Unbelievable. Heart-breaking. Whatever words we choose, they all fall far short of the reality. The loss of a child is a terrible thing. Written at the request of grieving parents and grandparents, *Shattered* has been called "one of the most comprehensive and practical grief books available." The book combines personal stories, compassionate guidance, and practical suggestions/exercises designed to help shattered hearts navigate this devastating loss. Honored as a 2017 Best Book Awards Finalist, *Shattered* became an Amazon #1 Bestseller soon after its release and has received sterling reviews by both mental health professionals and grieving parents. It is available in both paperback and electronic versions on Amazon and most other major online book retailers. For more information or to download a free excerpt, visit www.garyroe.com.

Heartbroken: Healing from the Loss of a Spouse

Losing a spouse is painful, confusing, and often traumatic. This comforting and practical book was penned from the stories of dozens of widows and widowers. It's simple, straightforward approach has emotionally impacted hearts and helped thousands know they're not alone, not crazy, and that they will make it. An Amazon Top 10 Bestseller, *Heartbroken* was a Finalist for two national book awards. Available in paperback and e-book formats from Amazon and most major online retailers.

Surviving the Holidays Without You: Navigating Loss During Special Seasons

This warm and intensely practical volume has been dubbed a "Survival Kit for Holidays." It has helped thousands understand why holidays are especially hard while grieving and how to navigate them with greater confidence. Being proactive and having a plan can make all the difference. An Amazon holiday bestseller, *Surviving the Holidays Without You* was honored as a 2016 Book Excellence Award Finalist. Available in paperback and electronic formats on Amazon and most major online retailers. For more information or to download a free excerpt, visit www.garyroe.com.

Saying Goodbye: Facing the Loss of a Loved One

Full of stories, this warm, easy-to-read, and beautifully illustrated gift book has comforted thousands. It reads like a conversation with a close friend giving wise counsel and hope to those facing a loss. Co-authored with New York Times' Bestseller Cecil Murphey, this attractive hardback edition is available at www.garyroe.com.

FREE ON GARY'S WEBSITE

The Good Grief Mini-Course

Full of personal stories, inspirational content, and practical assignments, this 8-session email series is designed to help readers understand grief and deal with its roller-coaster emotions. Several thousand have been through Good Grief, which is now being used in support groups as well. Available at www.garyroe.com.

The Hole in my Heart: Tackling Grief's Tough Questions

This easy-to-read e-book tackles some of grief's big questions: "How did this happen?" "Why?" "Am I crazy?" "Am I normal?" "Will this get any easier?" plus others. Written in the first person, *The Hole in My Heart* engages and comforts the heart. Available at www. garyroe.com.

I Miss You: A Holiday Survival Kit

Thousands have downloaded this brief, easy-to-read, and very personal e-book. *I Miss You* provides some basic, simple tools on how to use holiday and special times to grieve well and love those around you. Available at https://www.garyroe.com.

ONLINE RESOURCES

Gary Roe – Caring for Grieving Hearts

www.garyroe.com

GriefShare

www.griefshare.org

The Grief Toolbox

www.thegrieftoolbox.com

Open to Hope

www.opentohope.com

The Compassionate Friends

(for those who have lost children)

www.compassionatefriends.org

A REQUEST FROM THE AUTHOR

Thank you for taking your heart seriously and reading *Please Be Patient, I'm Grieving*. I hope you found some comfort, healing, and practical help in its pages. I would love to hear what you thought of the book. Would you consider taking a moment and sending me a few sentences on how *Please Be Patient, I'm Grieving* impacted you? Send me your thoughts at contact@garyroe.com. Your comments and feedback mean a lot to me and will assist me in producing more quality resources for grieving hearts. Thank you.

Warmly,

Gary

Visit Gary at www.garyroe.com and connect with him on Facebook, Twitter, LinkedIn, and Pinterest

Facebook: https://www.facebook.com/garyroeauthor

Twitter: https://twitter.com/GaryRoeAuthor

LinkedIn: https://www.linkedin.com/in/garyroeauthor

Pinterest: https://www.pinterest.com/garyroe79/

ABOUT THE AUTHOR

Gary's story began with a childhood of mixed messages and sexual abuse. This was followed by other losses and numerous grief experiences.

Ultimately, a painful past led Gary into a life of helping wounded people heal and grow. A former college minister, missionary in Japan, entrepreneur in Hawaii, and pastor in Texas and Washington, he now serves as a writer, speaker, chaplain, and grief counselor.

In addition to *Please Be Patient, I'm Grieving*, Gary is the author of numerous books, including the award-winning bestsellers *Shattered: Surviving the Loss of a Child, Heartbroken: Healing from the Loss of a Spouse*, and *Teen Grief: Caring for the Grieving Teenage Heart*. He has been featured on Focus on the Family, Dr. Laura, Beliefnet, the Christian Broadcasting Network, and other major media and has well over 500 grief-related articles in print. Recipient of the Diane Duncam Award for Excellence in Hospice Care, Gary is a popular keynote, conference, and seminar speaker at a wide variety of venues.

Gary loves being a husband and father. He has seven adopted children, including three daughters from Colombia. He enjoys hockey, corny jokes, good puns, and colorful Hawaiian shirts. Gary and his wife Jen and family live in Texas.

Visit Gary at www.garyroe.com.

Don't forget to download your free, printable PDF:

9 Principles for Caring for Grieving Hearts

https://www.garyroe.
com/9-principles-for-caring-for-grieving-hearts

Thanks for being patient with me. It means more than you know.

AN URGENT PLEA

HELP OTHER GRIEVING HEARTS

Dear Reader,

Others are hurting and grieving today. You can help.

How?

With a simple, heartfelt review.

Could you take a few moments and write a 1-3 sentence review of *Please Be Patient, I'm Grieving* and leave it on Amazon?

Just go find *Please Be Patient, I'm Grieving* on Amazon and then click on "Customer Reviews" just under the title.

And if you want to help even more, you could leave the same review on the *Please Be Patient, I'm Grieving* book page on Goodreads.

Your review counts and will help reach others who could benefit from this book. Thanks for considering this. I read these reviews as well, and your comments and feedback assist me in producing more quality resources for grieving hearts.

Thank you!

Warmly,

Gary

NOTES

NOTES

NOTES

NOTES

_____

_____

_____

_____

_____

_____

_____

_____

_____

_____

_____

_____

_____

_____

_____

_____

Made in United States
Orlando, FL
07 November 2021

10251357R00069